GROTESQUE TENDERNESS

Grotesque Tenderness

Daniel Cowper

McGill-Queen's University Press

Montreal & Kingston • London • Chicago

ISBN 978-0-7735-5627-0 (paper)
ISBN 978-0-7735-5770-3 (ePDF)
ISBN 978-0-7735-5771-0 (ePUB)

Legal deposit second quarter 2019
Bibliothèque nationale du Québec

Printed in Canada on acid-free paper that is 100% ancient forest free
(100% post-consumer recycled), processed chlorine free

We acknowledge the support of the Canada Council for the Arts,
which last year invested $153 million to bring the arts to Canadians
throughout the country.

Nous remercions le Conseil des arts du Canada de son soutien. L'an
dernier, le Conseil a investi 153 millions de dollars pour mettre de
l'art dans la vie des Canadiennes et des Canadiens de tout le pays.

Library and Archives Canada Cataloguing in Publication

Title: Grotesque tenderness / Daniel Cowper.

Names: Cowper, Daniel, 1981– author.

Series: Hugh MacLennan poetry series.

Description: Series statement: The Hugh MacLennan poetry series

Identifiers: Canadiana (print) 20190056355 |
Canadiana (ebook) 20190056371 | ISBN 9780773556270
(softcover) | ISBN 9780773557703 (PDF) | ISBN 9780773557710
(ePUB)

Classification: LCC PS8605.O93 G76 2019 | DDC C811/.6–dc23

This book was typeset by Marquis Interscript
in 9.5/13 New Baskerville.

to Emily Margaret

CONTENTS

PART III   A LITTLE HISTORY

PART IV   WINDFISHING

PART V   THE SALT WORLDS

PART I

The Life & Crimes
of
Sextus Tarquinius

Why should the worm intrude the maiden bud?
Or hateful cuckoos hatch in sparrows' nests?
Or toads infect fair founts with venom mud?
W. Shakespeare, *The Rape of Lucrece*

TRANSUBSTANTIATION

1936 / Paris

Radiation fills the pergola where Mother,
Father, Sextus, and his sister Netta

are templed on Sunday
in the Bois de Vincennes. Crowned

with rectrices and filoplumes, Sextus overlooks
Lac Daumesnil, Mother's lip-paint

remarking how pink boats
lump lakeskin to lenses, how cyclists click past

like frantic insects. Sextus watches Father prod
a notebook with castles, crows – the charcoal's scrape

mimicking claws of frisking sparrows. A pack
of baccalaureates assess the Tarquins

and back away, sneering:
Les juifs profifique, comme les rois d'antans

ont infesté le Bois de Vincenne.
Father winces. Mother smiles, lights

a Gauloise. *Tout ira mieux,* she assures, *en Pologne.*
Along the lakeshore herons tong

snakes from the reeds. Scaled tails whip,
rewrap beaks in coral loops

until their heads asphyxiate
in the birds' patient throats. Papa's crayon strokes

the page portraying a life-size sparrow.
He tears it out, tucks it in a crack: *Regardes, Sextus.*

A coriolis of house-sparrows side-eye, size up
and idolize Father's pale ikon. Wind fidgets the scrap

and the sparrow portrait wavers, self-animates –
thickens into depth and breathes, unfastens

from its sheet and flies into the rafters,
leaving that paper marked with random

smuts. When much older, Sextus would cringe
to think how sharply he saw that sketch

sublimate to feathered flesh and blood.
Mother shimmers in the green day

folding Netta's grudging fingers in her own:
Tout ira mieux, she intones, *en Pologne.*

PHORESY

1942 / Krakow Ghetto, Poland

Sometimes post-curfew in their canvas cots
Sextus and Netta stay up concocting

plots. *Looking for alien worlds to colonize,*
Netta whispers, *rockets are shot at distant stars*

leaving Dreadful Earth behind so fast
time nearly stops for those inside ...

In the Ghetto

days stick like wet pages. Soldiers patrol
street corners. Blood bubbles where bullets pass in.

Birds taste like what they feed on says Father,
snaring pigeons on ghetto windowsills.

Under flipped baskets captives fatten up on corn.
Chicken soup, bluffs Mother as she doles it out.

This can't last, Dad prays, bony hand on her belly.
Our next won't learn words for bayonet or bomb.

Sextus asks: *What do the Germans think we did?*
Father shrugs. *Someone should say we didn't*

the boy suggests. Then one day *Mother's gone,*
Netta's gone, Father sobs.

Heirlooms

evaporate. Father's hands always hunting for his.
Then: *I've paid someone to hide you. You'll leave*

tonight.
                              Father holds back the wire,
shoves Sextus through and stays behind, re-hooking

snipped filaments to hide the cut. *Be safe*
he blesses, and hurries off. Then the boy

wanders nocturnal boulevards spare
as interstellar gaps. Feral cats transit

the vacuum with him like rare asteroids, threshing
tails like space-dust behind them. The wakeful boy

aches alone till dawn and goes to meet Father
when frightened lines file out the Ghetto gates.

Piss off – I don't know you. Dad kicks
Sextus away and spits. Soldiers cram the men on trains

as from the PA Ilse Werner trills
"O mein Sohn." The engine carts its freight away.

Sextus finds the address, knocks. "Phoresy"
they call it, being fetched to a stone farmhouse:

four low walls with statuettes of Mary
holding candles. A milch cow and donkey

emit little sighs. *If soldiers come, get
in the woods.* Bible, fieldwork, rosary,

rest – never enough to eat. Father
breaks rocks at the Knochenmühle. Netta stacks

marionettes at Auschwitz. Mother's ashes
cycle mutely through the troposphere.

TOO SMALL TO EAT

1944 / Kleszczow, Poland

At dusk, necklaces of crows collect on girders
under the railway bridge. Sextus forages

through the overhung ravine, collecting dead birds
the rookery dumps out. Camouflaged in dry grass,

Sextus finds a sparrow. *Nothing eats them*
he muses, *they're too small.* Overhead, a train's approach

reverberates in the riveted guimbardes
of ironwork, mixes with what spills

from cattle cars: babies' caterwauls,
basses joined in *Barukh ata Adonai …*

a phrase of folksong. The boy squats, willing
himself not to cry, fills his ears by humming

harmony with metal larynges until the gully
stills. The train glides on. Thorns scratch nearby –

a mink-eyed girl confronting him
by fluke, her own pockets gnarled

with crows' claws. *I wasn't*, he hisses, *I was here …*
But the wild girl in her soldier's coat

flings gravel at his shins and runs. Later
Sextus dreams of catching her,

pinning the leshanki down, her naked breast
pink and glistening as raw birdsmeat

behind parted mats of feathers.
She blinks and whistles beneath his kisses

but something's weathered and jerking,
wet in her shuddering flesh. Pinions squish

to slimy lime as Sextus shivers awake
in his damp berth of blanket and leaves,

jaws clamped shut.
The meadow's balconies transmit

clipped ciphers from songbirds he loves
for being too small to eat.

CHILD'S PLAY

1959, Krakow, Poland

After the war, Netta sends cryptic
postcards from Paris. Dad brings home

Dola, his oak-toothed wife from Mauthausen.
Decrepit bohemians, Father and Dola

hole up in a Krakow tenement: eat
at whim, screw, lie in: suck respite

like sips of wine. At film school
Sextus's stunted cohort imbibes

dosages of Marx, applauds sermons
on "workers and peasants." Veterans

at escape, a generation's sooty eyes
fixate on exits.
     Hungry to play-fight

in this paused apocalypse, Sextus prowls
the "gods" in cinemas,

sits by single girls in paradise.
As the projector's beam spills its opal scenes

hands brush on the armrest, rub
wrists, mime cat's cradles,

revolve fingernails on stranger's palms – tenderly
grate fingertips up zippers. Too engrossed

in the film to kiss,
couples fondle each other

to stifled epiphanies while soundtrack
and shaft of light enact

their supple rites.
                    On summer days Sextus basks
at Kryspinów beach, chatting up bathers

whose limbs incarnate the Wiła
of Cannes or California. Being

undergrown reveals advantages:
schoolgirls too young to know

the blank affect prescribed by Soviet life
take Sextus for a boy their age.

Poland's damned, writes Netta from Paris.
Finesse a trip to France: when you arrive,

claim your French passport. Don't go back. Grief knots
Father's joints, seeps creased

in Dola's orbits and mammaries. Afraid to play
a dada part in Brezhnev's

Grand Guignol, Sextus slips offstage
as the murmuring house goes dark.

THE CAMERA

1963 / Paris

What can't the Camera record? Naked
reflection on lake water, hierarchy

of tadpoles exposed in Sextus's own outline; glare
without the faux-fantasy lens-flare; phantom

colours spawned outside colour-space;
simultaneous meaning; sheens too faint to see

except peripherally. The Camera
bears down on, obsesses over, depicts

parables of prey circling back while vampires
wait to welcome with a German kiss – skyscrapers,

gunslingers, scout leaders in Congress
denouncing greed. Gentlemen jewel thieves,

debutantes' faces fuzzed
to perfection, fear metamorphed

to rapture. *Lights? Camera?* and over drinks
the scared-to-displease actresses

angle for auditions. Later Sextus denudes them
and explores, magnifies their animal forms

till all he detects is caked grease and
glitter of stubble. His loss of sympathy

corresponds to the Camera's sacrament
as Betelgeuse's wavelengths

synchronize with the swinging tails
of men's seeds. Even the Camera's acolytes

wish its anonymizing gaze
would leave one beauty unframed

and ordinary despite longing
or exhaustion. Sextus aches for some face

immune to screen tests to keep
her quiddity mid-peeve or daydream:

covetable as Eve offering to share
ice cream. *Have you tried my favourite flavour?*

she'd invite, rendering up the chilly
see-through cup

beneath a painted tree.

FUGITIVES WILL BRING THE NEWS

1968 / Beverly Hills, California

Their guests draw close to the glow
loosed by Eve's slow furnace, her

flesh a space-age chassis shielding
hidden workings. Astronauts and novelists

worship her; after midnight, callers
leave without hats or coats, dazed

as sunbathers. Sextus finishes his morning coffee
at their kitchen table; a mermaid squirms in the dregs.

Each dawn of married life he cuts appleskin
to check if cinders fall out smoking – if she's

some crime he's charged with. Sextus walks to work
wondering whether to warn Eve how

if she turned to other men his basic
constants would de-calibrate – his stars

start blasting nuclear filth instead of light:
how hagfish and curious squid

would convulse as his gulfs
were saturated with the grief

she bred. Over his world's
wreck he'd brood, like a friable god

unable to abide the fickleness
of mortals or free will's vicissitudes.

Sextus walks home thrilled as a suitor
trysting with Eve on ground gummy

underfoot with offerings. He staggers,
stoned on their daring,

like a submersible diving to untested depths
while the ocean piles higher and higher.

NEWS

1969, London, England

Wet throbs burble in the wires as
transatlantic lines exchange their speech:

… Great – the baby's restless to be born. /
                                    I'll stay till Monday. /

In London? /
                        See some friends before I leave. /

Going out? /
                        I didn't think you'd mind. /

*Does it matter if I mind? I'll have some
friends round too, like Jay – he still adores me. /*

Do what you like, Sextus says, sick with himself
for not lying from the start. Contrite

next morning, he warms cocoa for the chic
gamine who'd clutched his arm at the Playboy Club, later

left a thorn of paraesthesia in the singing
sparrow of his crotch. She sits

on the kitchen stool, legs crossed,
cradling her croissant like a telephone. *Br-ring br-ring,*

she mocks, bites the horn away and smirks:
a refugee rusalka or film student from Paris,

it hardly matters. The phone
rings. *Sextus here. Yes, speaking.*

What do you mean she's dead?

                     Fissures in the weave,

chelicerae greedily
shredding the sacred tissue.

                What for? Macabre
questions like the lasso interrogating Eve

and Jay together? Eve's breast
sheared off like antique

statuary? The X-wound
incised on Eve's stomach

swapped for a soppy orifice
from which the coroner pried

their son, whose heart – had what?
beat on awhile

in the cooling womb
while killers arranged Eve's limbs,

dabbled like bad children
her blood on the walls? Eve's flesh

was set like concrete when they found it,
unique smoke

soaked back into the fabric.
In Sextus's ears a tuning orchestra of teeth

unclicking and closing, cats' jaws
ending the game with their prey.

ELECT

1969 / Spahn Movie Ranch, California

Out in the desert perelesnyks notch
bent crosses between their eyes. Dancing maenads

dodge drunks who clutch
at wave-soft tits and burp. Tabloids

blare: … *sexpot killed in horror scene …*
… *husband wept, say friends,* as if perplexed

between pity and scorn. *Pig*
smeared on the door in blood.

Funeral home to phone,
headstone to order. Eve's mother obsessed

with her ruined apparition, the unnamed
doll shape of the unborn boy. Airwaves whistle

over the corpses like grasshoppers: *cult*
orgy … underground porn … voodoo-fuelled …

Light pools in desert silos where
perelesnyks fumble with their New Age

facsimile of Nazism: plot to trigger
race wars, hallucinate how in the aftermath

the acid-dropping Elect will re-enslave
surviving blacks. Praying for Armageddon, they race

to slaughter enough hairdressers, enough leonine
heirs and daughters to glut their private myths.

MACBETH

1975 / Los Angeles

Forests of women surround his home.
Walking safe paths, Sextus overhears

a snigger and ... *Little Jew* he thinks they whisper,
chuckling over stories from his bed.

Girls of all sorts: Hugh Hefner's hand-arounds,
escorts, hippie divorcées, models

starving for debuts. Sextus picks out lisps
he's heard before, that bored him

after he'd filled a rubber or two,
tied off the squashy tips of goo.

Vanilla sex,

taboo, he boasts, *they queue up for more,*
keep score, memorize tidbits tabloids

might pay for – hound through drawers
like brides.

Filthy boy they mutter, *pathetic monster.*
As if they were surprised! Before the first

sea beast milted its harbour white, nuzzling
its snout on a screaming sacrifice,

the women knew. Aren't they all
monsters too? "So innocent! So young!"

Newsreaders cluck their tongues over candids
from New York to Timbuktu,

reporters call victims for interviews;
while Minotaur drools in his maze

the box office booms.
For Sextus, each
fresh transgression is a PR coup. The wood

of women thickens, its whispers increase
from day to day. New arrivals lick away

corned-beef lipstick and sound their horns.
None of them look like Eve. Where

do you hide a leaf? In a forest,
and a body in a forest of bodies. What

did Sextus try to lose, hurtling through
this underbrush of flesh?

NOTES FOR THE SENTENCING

1977 / Mulholland Drive

"When Lucretia arrived she looked like the boneless
parts of a hand pressed on a flashlight.

We shared a quaalude in my studio. Like ale clarified
with isinglass, as the chemicals took effect

they made her more translucent. Looking down at her
was like looking at you, Eve, through moving water

and she moaned *no* unfairly using your voice,
and *no* again, as if complaining to herself

like you would. I felt again the sunset
that coppered you and the madrona branches

that night we camped and fought in the uplands.
After our anger melted on our tongues like salt,

you and I lay down in a pile of arbutus leaves
and bark that crackled into anxious breath.

I wanted you but you turned away.
When I pulled you near you fought back

silently until I paired your limbs with my limbs
and made you couple with me. Even then you hissed

no to yourself, and *no* again,
until we flinted off a third heartbeat between us.

You held me while we started to overlap
in the fluttering thing that unfolded inside you.

I thought I smelt again spiced gasps of leaves and bark
leaning over this girl I wanted

who was sulky from being stoned
and somehow lit up with you.

After Lucretia left, saying nothing, I slept,
dreaming a thing that was dead

and had always been dead.
A face like peeled fruit and ribs

of long grey worms that snaked out blindly
locating what they liked by sense of touch."

PSYCHIATRIC EVALUATION

1978 / Chino Men's Correctional Facility

"Never been to a shrink before? Relax, Sextus.
When'd you start drugging girls for sex? You think

it up yourself? Drug your wife? Why not? Women
treat you funny, being small? Being famous?

Do you like your penis? What scares you?
Relax, Tarquinius. Tell me about your penis

I mean parents. Nazis gassed
your mom? War's malnutrition kept you

small? You can't escape it all,
even if you escape the worst. What do you like

about sedated girls? Does coitus
feel different when they're drugged, or

you want things they won't agree to? You find
young ones easy to boss around – they take

their clothes off when they're told?
Your dad and sister (sorry, half-sister)

survived the war. Why'd that dope cult
kill your wife? Full-term pregnant

when she died. Boy or girl? Your mom expecting
also when she died? Life stammers,

Tarquinius, some wombs chronically
miscarry. Story of your life? Why

weren't you home that night when junkies
knifed your wife? Balling one last fan

before fatherhood? Did you mean
to be faithful afterward? How many other girls

did you sedate? Lucretia wasn't the only one
or youngest, was she? And look: you've always

escaped the worst. Anything that lives
long enough survives itself, jettisons old shapes

on the benthos like caddisfly larvae.
Remember the little creatures morph

through several instars before they rise
on summer wings

to ovulate and die."

FAILURE TO APPEAR

1994 / Paris

Who'd Sextus hope to dupe, bragging
Lucretia was "not unresponsive" as if

the paired negations framed a crevice
he could sneak inside? As if he couldn't be refuted,

sued for assault – as if there weren't
other girls who could accuse. Only men so

self-delude: an orchid mantis knows
it can't eat light; mimic octopi

charading as scorpionfish
or crabs don't forget to ooze through any exits

bigger than their beaks.
Mimic, model, dupe. Who'd Sextus hoax

and why? *You always lie*, his father warned.
His life work's been suppressing

disbelief, fooling willing viewers
with practical techniques. In Paris

Sextus swaps his masquerade to meet
his fiancée's white dress, a tower

of cake. When asked, like a sad gossip
he confides Lucretia was "… regrettably not

unschooled in sex …" Something like a shrimp
chews out, supplants a tuna's tongue,

feeds on the host's prey pre-swallow,
lays eggs in the tuna's throat. Ecologists

swear nothing is wasted, each mangled
rabbit feeds an owlet. But

pain, that frantic poltergeist, feeds
nothing. Now he's a husband, father:

when Sextus's daughter asks if he raped
a little girl like her, how can he respond

except by yanking his shoulders up
till the tissue rips? Split from his torso,

Sextus's moulting arms and head would lift
off like a costume, the loosening skin

of his lower half fall down like baggy pants.
Callow and stinging he'd slither from that mess,

leave his hollow, cast-off self sloppily
insisting: "But it was not as they say."

THE FUGITIVES

2005 / Paris

Sextus's daughter plaits her mother's hair
on Sunday, shrined above Lac Daumesnil.

Below the Tarquins, duos in rented pedalos
progress in loops, while carp interpolate

wherever crumbs or loaf-ends fall.
Sextus's son caresses each line he draws,

admires his gothic spires. *Qu'est ce
dans l'ombres – des arbres? Et là,*

dans la main de la fille? Some tourists rubberneck
nearby, a tour-guide jerks his head. *Filmmaker,*

he points out, *the pedophile, a fugitive.* Sextus rises
to dissent, wanting to point at them

and shout: *Lucretia forgave me!
Has she forgiven you?* But already

they've moved on. Sextus looks back
to beauty: wife and daughter, son. A sparrow

rasps nearby. He portraits it mid-performance: tears
out the image for his son, who chinks the stiff

scrap between two stones in the windowsill,
as if perched there to sing. The Tarquins gather up

their things, head home. Excited by solar rays
the park's abandoned pedal-boaters

and bicyclists rise from rented thrones
to climb glassy switchbacks from flesh to void,

aerobatic as mating ephemera
flapping banners of pneumatic bone.

PART II

Regrets

Quand reverray-je, hélas, de mon petit village fumer la chemi-
née et en quelle saison reverray-je le clos de ma pauvre maison

...

J. du Bellay, *Les Regrets*, xxxi

THE LOTUS-EATERS

On clammy piers awaiting
day the herons hunker down.

Through gaps in coastal peaks, dawn
shocks her claques a panty-pink.

In cul-de-sacs, by beaded cars
left squatting by the curb,
striped thrushes stage their sieges on the lawn.

A working mom at morning mass
repents of rising early. Swathed

by a passing thurible in fumes, she fakes bland
prayer: between her folded palms

secretes a yawn. Aghast in the eastern window,
Mary-in-the-Stained-Glass lifts
to ruby lips a glowing hand.

In his dingy quad 'cross town
a college kid is reading Waugh,

jealous of mason's spires
and gowned tutorials.

Intincting toast in honey, he fingers
honey-textured words he's never heard,
coveting April "lancets" and amber "oriels."

At the municipal reservoir
silver snags pin back the bogs, rotting grass

clasps alder boughs and bullrushes.
The glottal call of a crake

knocks from reed beds
where lichened cedar trees stand rooted,
long drowned in the man-made lake.

Here, salmonberries droop
last summer's fruit, and civilization

gives way to wetland, layering
new and old like spirit and flesh.

Trailing fine threads behind us
like deserting sailors, we're tied

to distances we do not know.

COUNTERPOISED

In December damp I head out for a row,
sliding my tin boat into the slot of water
where a creek bevels the shore's gravel
and ocean unravels the creek's flow.

Rock and keel grate as I push off from shore,
scudding down the drowned stream bed
where, in the winter-clear water, discreet fish dart
and flags of seaweed sway a futile semaphore.

Twisting on their rowlocks, oars pleat
the surface into whirls like spinning whelks
as I swing from my bay where tilting hemlocks
soften the air with creaks and sighs like felt.

Beyond their shelter, in the world of the winter sea
the wet air scrapes my knuckles at each stroke.
Out on the indifferent water, I sing the old carols,
hymning their landscape of shepherds and belfries.

An archipelago of seals spectates in silence,
mute as buoys until they lose interest, and bow
back to their hemisphere, chivvying greenling
through ropes of kelp hung counterpoised in the currents.

Back in the bay, I beach and debark. My feet
buckle sand and the keel grinds barnacle casks
as I drag the boat to grass. Uphill, the holly berries
in the wood stove keep their husks of ruddy heat.

DEPARTURES

The day you left our island you looked back
when the ferry started: you watched the zinc-capped pilings
shudder in the churning wash. But you wanted
to inherit the old world, to live with its stonework
and history: escape the lackadaisical
attitude of home.

Now I'm on the ferry too, after a weekend back.
I have to catch an early flight out east
to Toronto's collage of enclaves
where I have a basement suite
and a job helping businessmen
raise capital, close deals, defend.

This white ferry slides through daylight
that's already texturing our island
and peeling off the morning's residue
in fiddleheads of steam. In the mountains' shelter,
a rind of night melts slowly.
And the boat's full, as it is every morning,

of people who've known us since childhood.
As the screws grind toward that cooler
flank of the inlet, I regret my own exile.
I grieve for both of us, and all the others
who've claimed the heirlooms of Europe,
or new friends at American colleges

or the abrupt adulthood of the oil patch.
We've all tried to become someone novel
at a safe distance from the embarrassments of youth.
But you and I are getting too old to ignore
the homesickness that burdens us,
the way the beaded spring and autumn moisture

weighs down the fringes of the hemlocks.

BALLGAME

Kids with foul balls retrieved from briers
are pleading for payment
but the scorekeeper's

beaking umpires

while her friends laugh
and jeer. Two drunks clang
empties on warped chicken wire.

The pitcher leaves the rubber, slowing
the game's pulse.
Swallows scythe in the outfield

where wild daisies are growing.

Overhead, twin
contrails snell the cold
ailerons of a Boeing.

RAT PATROL

Alliance Township, Alberta

Coyote tooths the shell of spring snow
mouthing fluff and a squeaking tongue of blood.
Coyote scans the firn patch, swallowing,
when boys yip through the morning airflood,

and Coyote shades to cover. Two boys
arrive with baseball bats –
looking for an untouched lobe of snow
near mouse-frass in the turf. *Rats* –

*Just field mice – Rats I said, we're the rat
patrol.* The first boy slams his stick
in the snow and mice
stream out the sides slick

as marbles. *Look!* one yells
and clubs. *There! There!*
they chatter, smacking the bare turf,
crushing mice until the prairie air

whiffs sour with offal and mashed grass.
They trample the next snow pad, flushing
mice out from underfoot like water drops
they swat into the sod, mushing

underheel the last twitches
from snapping bones. One boy, worn out,
picks a mouse up tailfirst,
flips it to the other, who swings his clout

but only clips the mouse. *Foul ball,*
the batter calls out, *Fuck it all,*
another's tossed by the tail – hit hard,
ripped apart with a small

dark spurt. The boys
leap up and whoop.
One picks up another corpse,
slings the messy sop

at his friend. It smears his right cheek red.
Gross you sicko: flings one back.
The boys whip mice and dodge
until, pitching arms slack,

they share a drink. Sucking in
drool for the carrion gleaning
he's leaving, Coyote jogs
out the draw, his alien-to-meaning

anima unsettled. Totem of jokester,
double-crosser, he unsmells bloodscat,
unhears berserk laughter, barking cries.
Digs up last week's calf head, intact

except cheekmeat, tongue, and eyes.

RED-EYE

Other passengers recline
their seats –
we'll land at Pearson
before the workday starts.

I set my watch ahead
from ten to one, the night cut short.
We're rushing east
like arterial blood.

Something blank's down there.
I can't make out
the familiar motley
of mountains and Mandelbrot ravines.

Lights prickle out. Occasional
beads of fire flicker
as if on fishing line.
Cars streak down country roads

like comets chasing their tails.
Some unmanageable
organism animates these radiances,
elevates this vessel,

metabolizes fiat currency
and rare earth metals, mandates
we delete a nominal hour from life
each time zone it drives us east.

SPANDREL FOR PAN TWARDOWSKI

Spooked gulls pull loose from their trajectories,
peeling shoreward. At the inlet's mouth,
storm clouds knock closer,
crackling like far-off falling scree, but the low
sun still bares itself for the skin-soft lee
my boat skims.

Noiseless lights needle off the water and in shock
I cut the engine. The hull
rocks to a halt
in a strange forest of spider-threads: spiderlings,
alarmed by storm-shudders,
abseiled from their silken kites and settled here

by chance. Sunlight chases up abandoned threads
the way high beams
run down power lines at night.
I recall the Polish Faust, how the God
of second chances left him gangling
in the clouds alone

till judgment day. The lonely sinner learned
the speech of a spider he found in his sleeve,
guarding an egg-bundle. When it hatched
he was foster-father to her clutch. In goose-summer,
the Poles say
Faust's spiders are fetching news

of world affairs for their friend. But I know
newborn wood spiders climb stalks of grass
and spin silk kites to catch updrafts
over mountains or out to sea.
And whatever they mean
in Krakow,

here each thread means
flimsy legs
are dimpling the surface tension of the sea.
They mean, when hearthsmoke starts to brown
the seaward sky at dusk, my porch
will be sewn in with silk

till someone takes a stick and cuts them down.

A LONG COUNTRY

Past a streetlamp in Toronto my
shadow wheels aside while
my next shadow – as if someone's catching up –
overtakes, dimming also

as it shrinks from its replacement.
Why'd I come east? Back home
islands throw patches of darkness shoreward
sobering their eastern sides with shade

but Toronto's snow in unbruised parks
and car dealerships reflects arclight
on the cloud cover; bright patches
of stooped sky flag every spot

that's fenced off or abandoned
as if Toronto sprayed glow-in-the-dark
on shy kids at its party. I know
the national myth that we belong

to winter, but I'm sour as an expat
when I see glare doubled on the clouds, or
sidewalks manufacturing shadows,
or brake lights swimming by in ruby shoals.

UNDERGROUND

Strap-hanging in a subway car
with other commuters,
swaying. Bumping hips
like pickles shaken in a jar

at each bend. Wheels abrade the air.
Jiggling portraits on plexiglass show
men and women mulling plans
and cross-appeals, or staring

at phones pastel-backed as duotangs.
Then a voice from the emptiness outside:
Call that gandy dancing, dog-fuckers?
I'm starving, so big-cat and bang

it down. Cackles vibrate in the crypt
we're traversing, skeletal limbs scrape
closer in the surrounding dark.
Then steel clangs and treads grip

gravel. Halogen lights flare
on the tunnel roof. Slowing, our capsule
nears a hollering foreman and his crew.
And we were never scared –

never felt the cold slop of panic
in forgotten organs. Our ghosts
debunked, we grip harder
what's trained and automatic.

Wind whistling through plastic fencing
zap-strapped on rebar
stakes, or a sheltered robin, calling and calling?
Maybe that fluctuating roar

is an airplane starting its descent, or
factory-sharp leaves flailing
anger from the air?
The screech and rumblings of the gale

blend into the city's answering crush
and trash as smoothly as a shout in a stairwell
blurs into its echo. Why haven't I
seen this before? I've passed concrete walls

without noticing their ivy
ransacked by starlings for fruit;
without seeing gulls drain beachward for the night
while bank-towers throw sunset back and forth.

SNAKE IN THE MIND

The serpent's deep-sea stench
scrapes barnacles and bladderwrack

on treebark. Fat lips work slow,
gulping air how fish

gulp water, as the firwood
drums with the snake

thudding into tree trunks.
Stubborn branch-stubs

in a fallen abattis
punch holes in the worm's blundering skin.

It struggles on, smearing a white paste
behind it like rancid crabmeat.

I run and run. At home, I hide
in the darkness of a kitchen cupboard

but the snake is already there.
How'd you get here before me? I ask

as oozing coils thicken and unwind.
Before you, the serpent says, *I waited a long time.*

TIME DELAY

In Toronto, ice-dust in the air bends haloes
around streetlamps,
and the side streets are lined with sooty berms
of shrunken ice.

But I miss the western spring
that's opening back home –
the eucalypt wind, rain playing
its quick carillon on the sea –

creeks clattering down rusty couloirs
above the highway, pebbling
through the chicken wire. Tongues of silt
lapping the pavement.

At home, copper fluff's on the sword ferns –
catkins dangle on the alders,
loose with dust –
the horse-pasture's flocked with thrushes.

But I'm not home. I won't be home
till paired swallowtails helix
between the broadleafs, and hummingbirds
gem on the hemlocks' tassels.

I'm stuck in Toronto till the students
dump their semester's furniture on sidewalks,
and cicadas buzz over back streets
like faulty transformers.

WALKING

Awhile tonight I've tried
to keep in the rut, not trip.

Sometimes cedar branches
flip underfoot, swiping my shins.

A stream's unburdening itself. Overhead
a split tree's squealing in the wind.

By these boundaries I wayfind. No
stars, front windows, or even light-leak

from pulp mill or city street
bleaches the sky. My feet

have to feel their way
by the caked mud of the rut

and it's too dark to tell
if my eyes are still open or shut.

SECRET WATER

For Dr T. Rubin

Trying not to stare
I watched light-reeds
snap and spin away
under shelves of antique periodicals.

We met again years later,
hiking off-trail
where January clinked
through narrow cracks.

We spooked a late-season fawn
from his den: born
scrawny, born to starve, he
skittered away over the rot-soft duff.

Lake ice crosshatched
indigo reflections.
Golden reeds jumbled
on the floor. In specific altitudes

alder sticks bloomed
with silver floss – hairs of ice
excreted while freezing
from the deadwood's pores.

The soft frost
came off in your hand
and would have deformed
to moisture but you blew

the ice-pappi away
spinning through pipes of sun
like, you said, dandelion fluff
from a dandelion clock.

VAGRANTS

Last night I walked past tony boulevards
where arc lamps fluoresced
through glassy leaves, to the dead zone
by the port. Outlined by orange skyglow, a forest

of power lines tendriled above the alleys.
A girl stood by the curb, kitty-corner,
bundled up in fleece. She saw me looking,
smiled, and waved me over.

Not buying, I walked on. Some guy
weaved past me like a sailor still legged to his ship's
roll. A bubble of diseased flesh
squeezed out the corner of his lips

as he nodded kindly. Then I walked
alone where homeless stars
staggered along the sidewalks or sprawled
in doorways and burnt-out cars.

The stars were given up and grimy from drugs
or illness, weather – all three. *Some change today?*
one called, *A nickel? Thanks, brother.*
How 'bout another for the highway?

Too spaced or proud to panhandle, binners
hauled clinking carts along their route,
ignoring me and the other stars.
Muttering through fogs of hostile throats, or mute.

Help me out, a straggler begged, blue eyes
in twitching skin. *Help a brother out in Jesus' name.*
I'm freezing to death out here and I got
nobody, and nobody to blame.

At dawn the stars left, one by one,
to sieve the morning commute, or get their meds.
I walked home beneath my own street's oaks
watching dropworms blown in orbits on their threads.

CIVIL WAR

The day after blood in the city square
she stared across empty fields,
recalling how anger and prayer
were broken by nightsticks on plexishields

and gunshots. Flesh flexed within
her stockings as she leaned
through locust-song
and lavender. Little ants pinned

her lemon scarf and sleeves.
                          An unmarked van
          split flaps of living leaves,
          nosing from highway to lane.

Ants clicked on the windshield,
living hail rough wipers smeared
to paste while the driver swore,
geared down, and peered

ahead. Soldiers jostled in the back,
joking about kinds of gun,
slapstick deaths.   She heard the van
through the morning hum,

while field spiders
wove their lines
from awning to wall,
from rosehips to spines.

The van swung into view.
Bemused she watched a spider float on the air,
gold legs spread as if scared stiff.
Time combed out its hair.

Soldiers slid back the doors like tradesmen
unloading at a job site.
She waited between rows of lavender
for shots to cavity her meat,

opening in the heat like ears.

CROWSNEST PASS

Perched on their fieldstones and fenceposts
birds haven't yet found this doe's
corpse. But when the first vulture
falls from its thermal and crows

follow, charring the branches, beaks
will awl her gut and find
the furred limbs and sealed face
of the fawn she held five months and failed

to birth.
                    And in some gully the buck who sired
that fawn unfelts new antlers on a pine.
This death means no more to him than clashing
in the rut would've meant someday, with the honey-tined

soare that fawn would have become. And indifferent
beaks will clip away twined flesh
until the scraped mesh of doe's ribs
and finer cage within are dragged apart.

HOME BEFORE DARK

The inlet's snow-bound shores
are blue with dusk;
the flat horizon's doused the sun.
On the dock, tracks

rumple pale blue into bowls of shadow.
Turtle-backed dinghies
hunker in their cups of snow.
One cup's empty. Overhead

tideline-covering fir boughs
bend under ricks of powder,
until their burdens slough off,
tiling the shorecalm below

with scales of floating frazil ice.
Air hisses from the melting slush,
audible in the shelter of branches
and snowfall's hush.

And the rower pulling homeward
waits to hear that icy breath
against his dinghy's bow,
sliding nearer to its berth.

But still far from shore he only hears, stroke
after stroke, droplets flung out from oar-blades
and the ruffled wake behind the stern
rearranging its folds.

PART III

A Little History

Woe is me! I am undone,
for I am a man of unclean lips,
and I dwell in the midst
of a people of unclean lips.

Book of Isaiah 6:5

AGE OF INNOCENCE

We woke, heard Mum and Dad singing, snuck out
to watch them dance. Spotting us

they emptied homemade vino
on our heads, rubbed it in, rinsed

it out with more. Dad's beard smelt warm.
Mum went barefoot in our moon-wet

orchard. Both laughed as they swamped
us in yellow wine.

                  That was then: no rules except

        Be good.
             Unsupervised, we kids
squeezed through otters' dens, plucked

old wren nests like puffy cheeks
off twigs. We spooked nighthawks drowsing

in day-baked bracken, stroked the inflating
and deflating flanks of snakes in the dozy

grass.
                Less sleeping now, less dreaming.

After naps we swapped visions, spoke of

suns splitting in two at dawn to deasil the sky
on mirrored arcs, remerge at the far

horizon. There were always more apples
to peel, more trout to hook in the clay-banked

creeks.

> We get used to the basement
> apartment, to sirens and headlights

> crossing twill curtains as books on tape talk
> us to sleep. Floors creak overhead. Tape seals

> panes of spidered glass. Why'd we leave
> our orchard? We were still children then,

> doing what we were told. My brother
> and I fight over what to watch, who'll play

> on the PC. We live like that. Skate
> behind the strip-mall. Feed M&Ms to rats.

AGE OF EXPERIENCE

Following the retreating shore, we lead
our horses into valleys flat with slopped

deposits of silt and junk. Nail-toothed eels loop
in pools; huge squid ooze aimless around

the oily iridescence, skins rippling with
rainbow eyespots. While the earth drains we eat

those freaks, slice chunks off suckered arms.
The topsoil bakes with trapped compost

of choked sealife, drowned birds and beasts. Steam vines
up mountain slopes, crystallizes at night

on summits of rock. Boys track our plows,
sowing the exothermic plain. Girls pick

skulls from furrows instead of stones, parse bones
as beast or human. Skeletons stack neatly

into fences, white walls for huts. We wear
ourselves out working, dream *ad idem*

                              of mushy spatter

                              and drip on decking.
            Constant roll   of a wooden hull.

                                        Greedy water
                                        discs our sleep,

                    tossing up   little dollops
                    wherever   raindrops fall.

                                        Immense chime
                              of rain perforating the sea.

In my bunk, I listen to the hum of ants
hollowing ribs and tibia

within walls, admire
the myriad spider webs.

Through gaps between femurs and funnels
I watch insomniacs stumble

side to side in nocturnal fields, teasing
bones from rancid mud,

mourning over drowned unknowns,
the disarticulated dead.

                                    On the sea's tympanum
                          once we found a flotilla of glass buoys,

                            knitted in teal fibres of fishing nets.
                    Under them hung strips of over-weighted mesh,

                                snagged and tangled with dead
                                      sharks and cormorants,

loose sneakers and cushions.
On one stray cord a bride

in ivory gown
was leashed head downward

in the water, veil
and chiffon train

beating with an inorganic pulse.

AGE OF EXPLORATION

Strange place to visit, that town,
but there was nowhere else to go. We made
a joke of it, laughing as we rode in

at the boy jerking off out a window
onto grinning youths, their tongues
flicking like geckoes'. We shrugged off

touchy locals, the way they talked
as if brothels were charities. *Lotta widows move here
for work*, they insist. *Lotta kids kicked outta*

homes. Lotta orphans, nowhere to go.
An economy of last resort, a buyer's market.
Their polis respects bad endings, is grateful

for failure. Each street-corpse gets embalmed
on the public dime: carefully maquillaged
in a scarlet coffin. At the Beast

with Two Backs, a chalk-white donkey chases
sows till one, plied with beer,
gets too drunk to dodge his prodding, and

there's a round of whisky on the house.
Contortionists busk on wooden rostra, pushing
endless beads into rectums,

twisting dildos with their teeth. Everyone
wants to visit once, to see.

We hear wild reports
after the city burns, fairy tales of ifrits

or freak lightning, a fanatical posse
of prudes. Most say one man
torched himself and the notion spread.

Mass hysteria took hold, citizens
set fires to immolate their rivals
or families. Rioters nursed infernos,

ignited blocks at random – a street rave
nonpareil till highs wore off and heat
drove revellers into surrounding hills.

Small groups ringed the burning town,
drinking and whooping when gas stations
erupted parachutes of flame.

As embers furred to ash that ring
of watchers fell silent, realizing they had
nowhere else to go. Some stayed

in those hills reminiscing,
missing the good old days as time
transfigured them to sticks of dirt.

Crows skipped in the old camas field, uprooting
indigo blooms, twisting bulbs

from soil. We admired their antics – we had
flour by then, fresh bread. But the fishery

scared us: June's salmon were gone
zombie, rotten as kelts before they bumped

ashore. Eagles glutted on grey spoils
lipping streams. Sea stars and limpets,

rugs of mussels died off, disrobing rocks. Shore-wolves
digging for geoducks scrawned to stick figures,

disappeared into woods. We still had timber
to trade, shipped dry goods from Seattle. But ravens

attacked our docks en masse, tore burlap
apart in the stevedores' hands. At bakeries, crows

hopped past closing doors and flapped
in a frenzy from loaf to loaf, pecking

and shitting. Half the homes were nailed up
by September. On the first frost a herd

of cow elk ran up Granville, were trapped
by a following pack of bull elk, racks

and muzzles plastered black. Bull elk
hemmed their targets in, gored bleating cows

with blackened tines and stamped them down.
The chiselled teeth of males closed hungrily

on female throats and loins. Male elk
milled about that charnel street, grunting

and manic – tearing loose thick strips of flesh,
gulping hot mouthfuls of meat. After

that spectacle we all got out: took highways east.
In the Rockies we joined crews building

the railway. Pay was sachets of prairie grain,
silvers dollars mixed in the bags. In passes,

snow covered track beds as we worked. Snow fell
like we'd never seen, in white leaves. Frost

grew like fish bones on the ground. In Alberta
foothills we mended ranch fences,

worked oil fields when we could. No one liked us.
We were on edge. Too fervent: credited

ghost stories. Believed the woods were full
of kids lost in whiteouts, lying

in wait under wrappings of snow
for the next Chinook to wipe them bare.

I hear he's overdosed, gone
cold with the needle glued

in basilic vein. I drink from a cup
of tiny frogs – flinching toes

the temperature of water.
The first suicide I know has been depressed
for years, a troubled boy. He's tried before.

The next is unemployed, newly dumped,
on codeine.

Explicable sorrow,

we hope.
Pockets crinkle with dead lice,
homes waft with poison.

Imperceptibly the stories

stop making sense, shared over funeral
coffee that sticks to lips, stinks of rust

and rotten fish.
Lifeguards exsanguinate
themselves in public pools, schoolboys lie down

in front of buses. A baseball team
chugs antifreeze, winds up

littered on the field. None of it feels
real. Sweeping up dead bugs

takes all day, every venue's booked
for memorials. Parents break out with boils from guilt

or stress. Even animals go berserk: wasps
swarm baby strollers, rattlesnakes chase girls

in schoolyards. I hear farmers are slaughtering
livestock, shellacking barns with blood

to scare off death. Terrible storms batter
down power lines, hailstones crack windshields.

And boys keep dying. Finally, families with sons
still alive pack what they can in trucks

and drive west, over the mountains. Headed
nowhere special,

                              not coming back
                              till it's safe, or never.

A LAND FLOWING WITH SILK
AND MONEY

We travel by convey, tracking canyons west
with our expedition. Some mornings our hunters

bring back rabbits, a quartered deer, young
smallpox survivors from local tribes.

                                          Our fathers

      make those kids bear freight, chain them up
       like mules.
    Some say we saved them. Some say

the villagers are dead or drunken,
hardly notice when their children are snatched

by moonlight, brought gagged to our camp's nightly
column of fire. At dawn that flaming sentinel cools

to mist, snakes ahead of us down canyons,
always west. Where's it taking us? Why's it

guiding us at all? What waters down the smoke
each day, until we can hardly see it? That fog

evaporates when we arrive at grey beaches
sharped with logs.

In the greasy surf, our captives

squat in chains, hide eyes behind their palms
and die. Skins of sea creatures swaddle

their floated bodies in the tide: skins
of bears with fins, smooth-skinned fish

with bison's eyes and horns, bird skins
big as men.
                                        Without slaves

we didn't build to last.
Our boarding houses
crumble, peppered with fruiting mould.
Around our docks, you still spot

massive skuas massacring rock doves,
roosting on crooked rooftops. In this

town we watch storms lick mountains
to sand, prove

                    entropy's almighty. I

hope I didn't sell my soul, or if I did
it wasn't just for this.
                                        We never miss

the supple tree of smoke that led by day,
the radiant bar of fire that stood by us at night.

AGE OF PROPHECY

Self-appointed prophets screech
from construction cranes, climb billboards
for future condos. They cackle, garble
aposematic warnings. Tears

hiss in the blue flames streaming
from their lips. So sad, nearby

commuters can hear their skins
crackling, cooking on the inside
like microwaved chickens. But we like priests
to have their schtick together, slick

podcasts, personal stylists. We like
preachers who say *These are*

the good times, the years
of getting along. We're fond
of SUVs wrapped in a photoshopped
headshot, tagline in a readable font.

I'm always busy at the office,
reading up on sports concussions, waiting

for AI to save us. *Sustainability,* we sloganize,
Each generation richer than the last!
Each house bigger than the one knocked down!
Why not? With enough solar cells,

we'll all be idle, living off
the robots. Doomsayers plague patios

and diners, hassling pairs meeting up
off Tinder. The prophets stutter, work their jaws
as if about to spit. Nod. With every word
they speak, their whiskers

smoulder, blue flames in their mouths
and noses edged with rose.

AGE OF EMPIRE

When state radio comes in, we learn
what we're doing wrong. Prim accents explain
speaking Chinook is barbaric, the Kanakas
cheap labour, Japanese fishermen   worse than thieves.

We're eager to shape up. Someone says they've
passed a law   so we paint everything with blood: slop
blood on sidewalks with mops,   spray
it under bridges from boats.   Abattoirs

work round the clock, shipping full tins
to keep us going.   Ants
form chain gangs, chipping at clots.
Flies multiply, orgasmically suckering

each surface. Lynxes trot uneasily
through alleys,   tracking the ubiquitous
stench. New statutes are rumoured
hourly: bills insisting we   utter words

in alphabetical order,   wear watches
to measure how time gets used.   Media
outlets aggregate hearsay, publish op-eds
on playing along. What's permitted,

what criminal?   *Why worry,*
some ask. *The Crown's so far away. If we
can't check the laws, how can they watch
us?* Useful advice, but   we're

too buzzed to listen,   inventing new ways
to shame our neighbours. Our scabbed windows
glow red at night, adorning our skyline
like a thousand injection wounds   on ecstatic skin.

AGE OF SCIENCE

That night the stars didn't come out,
one by one. Astronomers on TV said

our universe was filled with dead
coals spinning down a dark stream,

their usual rates unchanged. Over St John's
dawn's final bloom blinked to black. *Why* we asked

in the private dark. Afraid to be alone
we met by lamplight, trading stories:

Sin of Man was one,

Age of Science, another. More

prayers than answers. Drowned men shivered
up beaches blue-lipped and hypothermic –

rocks haemorrhaged archaic corpses who ran
scared from sirens wailing above traffic.

Hotel lobbies overflowed with flustered
cadavers who'd found their old homes occupied.

My sister rushed up, garish with undertakers' rouge.
Eyes still bloodshot from formaldehyde

she cried aloud in some musical lexicon
like birdspeech. I loathed myself

puking when I tried to talk. We were all like that.
Roadsides stank of graves and stomach acids,

grievers sicking up in corners. Strange
creatures were sighted licking the sidewalks.

We slunk to bed. Rainfall
grained the morning when we woke and

Sin of Man wailed some headlines;

Age of Science soothed the rest.

PART IV

Windfishing

Fear only the red-gold sun with the fleece of a fox
Who will steal the fluttering bird you hide in your breast.
Fear only the red-gold rain
That will dim your brightness, O my tall tower of the corn,
You – my blonde girl …

E. Sitwell, "The Youth with the Red-Gold Hair"

1400 CROMIE RD

Pink with fuchsias, hanging baskets
vibrate on their wires. On the stovetop
an overfull kettle's not singing but sobbing

hot splashes of water. Cracked tiles mark
where in a fight over dishwashing
one boy slung a skillet at his sister. Quietly

the kettle tongues into teapot;
fermented screws of tea re-soften
to leaves in the circling current. A towelled girl

sprints down the hall. On cool
flooring between shower and bedroom door
her footprints shrivel

back to air. Trapped steam beads
on the bathroom ceiling. Spindly
arachnids gantried on the plaster

suckle on growing droplets before
the swelling, merging globes abscise
their surplus to the floor.

EUCLID REFUTED

She laughed, rosed by the driftwood fire,
tugging off her clothes till free:

then she owled down the night
beach and splashed into the sea.

We fondled flakes of phosphorescence
while a sailboat's swinging cable

belled on its mast in time to the sea
and she said she wasn't able

to *feel like that* for me. Before bed
I chose to forget her. So what'd I dream?

A botched kiss: our mouths unsure,
our fingers numb. Now angles spliced awry

don't sum to shapes. Names won't clothe
their wearers, nor disproofs falsify.

LABOUR DAY

Our hayfield and picnic blanket;
seascape
of quilled islands;

musical wine bottle; rumpled
eggshells.
Out on our dimpled sea

sailboats saunter
goosewinged under the crayfish sky.
Don't lift

your head just yet:
stay like this for a little while
watching kinglets

tumble through the cedar trees.
For just a little longer,
let me stir your strings

of autumn leaves.

GOODNIGHT, SEPTEMBER

Leaving you late through driveway shadows,
I look back at the clenched light
of your kitchen. You rinse our mugs alone,

moving with the grace of the unwatched.
Reflections varnish your side of the windows
so all you see glancing out

are portraits of yourself. You crook your head
in the glass, assessing the lines of your
likeness's throat. When my car starts

you come to the window,
lean in until your reflections
dim to transparency and you see me.

Mist grows on the cold
surface between our smiles
where your breath flowers against the glass.

You back away but I watch
those petals finish unfolding and vanish
before driving the dark roads home.

WEEKNIGHT

Where are you going
through cat-thin corridors?

Why pick your way
from parquet to parquet

between unworn shoes
and dirty clothes?

Don't dodge our card stand
over the Ikea ottoman

to move from bleached to black.
Stay within reach.

If you must go, we will walk together
from well-lit streets

to trees' shadows
piercing the wiry plenum of raindrops

and bursting wet spiderwebs
with our faces. We'll tire ourselves out

confronting headlights
of passing trucks and circle back.

Dark-winged cedars are flocking
by the lakeside: goffered
with oar-feathers of sun,
cantilevered

over the shoreline like cormorants
sunning their wings. Sick of walking
this loop with me, you stayed home. Overhead
crisscrossed limbs are tangled, locking

in a mesh. Wind flowing through
this weir of plashed branches stirs
the boughs, and bark rubbing against bark
whistles and chitters like a grove of birds.

Where branches chafe, their woolled grooves
(rawed tyee-pink) chirp and keen till grosbeaks
and siskins respond, mistaking
the cedars' twitters and squeaks

for birdsong. And maybe we've made
the same mistake. Maybe we're
no more alike than the songbirds
and the cedar weir.

VANCOUVER CHERRIES

Cherry branches anemoning from
a pollarded trunk
arc under heavy pebbles of rain
their spoon-shaped petals can't release.

The bones of new condos cast
shade and glare through November fog.
Halogens whine in corners
while heater-fans waltz on their wheeled skirts
trying to cure freshly poured cement
despite dampness in the air.

FINISTERRE

The last weekend we spent by the sea,
you hardly seemed there,
sleeved in our sheets at the B&B
or out with the wind in your hair.

We jawed back and forth without saying the things
we meant to say. You talked shop –
I named the auks and sanderlings.
Neither of us brought those questions up.

Loitering, lunching along the seawall,
we threw the seagulls our slices of peach.
We watched the clouds curdle into another squall,
and breakers hissing up and down the beach.

On the train ride home, the rail car rattling along,
I was stung by how you borrowed my pen
with a smile as if nothing was wrong.
The next day, I never saw you again.

After a line by G.K. Chesterton

Unless winter vents its grievances
in snow and pale blades of ice
ridge red shoots of maple
it isn't spring.
Spring is never spring

unless it comes too soon.
Unless male grackles, newly
iridescent and creaking in their mesh of oaks,
are smudged against the sky
by a freezing storm, it isn't spring.

Unless bracken ferns spooling
translucent life from warm soil
are killed with frost
and jellied by thaw, it isn't spring.
Spring wouldn't be spring if it didn't come too soon.

Back then, we were both too young.
Like duffers too shy with the tiller
we let our bowsprit luff
into the wind until our sails
cracked angrily in folds.

TOGETHER STILL

With nothing
left to say we breakfasted early
over our phones.

You told me
longbows made of yew

killed horsemen miles away.
*Those mountains across the water
mean something,* you said –

*Each an oreoglyph
in the sentence running south.*

I asked if you knew
the French for *yew* is *if.*
We glanced at the glow

behind the eastern mountains,
hoping for dawn to skew

its Jacob's ladders down
between the peaks.
You know when, looking down a cliff,

you feel the edge tug?
Your tea dregs spattered bars of dead bamboo

as logs of sunlight
thundered down the chutes.

An anemic dawn was seeping through the park
when I woke up and saw the snow.
Outside my window, maples who'd sighed
with leaves the day before were silent. Sheaves

of red and yellow trembled, here and there,
under the whiteness they cupped. Last night's leaves
were scattered on the new snowskin: lemon, orange,
blood-orange where they melted in.

It was the first snow – my annual seance with the past.
In the afterglow of first snowfalls, faces gloom
to expressions my first love made; women I pass
on the sidewalks accidentally ape

the shy and swivel of her gait.
Six winters have fallen now, one by one
since the night we watched the first snowflakes
swirl through globes of arclight,

standing together on the asphalt's shoulder.
First snow found us first on that lonely highway,
heading home after a midnight stroll.
Our breaths first feathered the darkness

together that night, as winter and fall overlapped
like tinted lenses. Each year since, I've been dogged
by her shade reaching out, repeating old accusations,
while overhead the shivering red

and gold-paned leaves unsheave
in the falling snow like startled flocks.
So I went to the park this morning
to meet her. But no voices called,

no accosting hands uncoiled against me
except the long-fingered cold.
Grey-barked trees leaned forward, instead,
quivering in the wind like patient hounds.

Goodbye, Romans said at interments,
Goodbye, and Goodbye. Hired clowns
imitated the dead, mocking
and reminding among the mourners.

I moat myself with winter sea,
I bury myself in woods.

Could I reworship the griefless minds
I knew in childhood?
Mink killing chickens for pleasure and practice;
otters deboning their flounders alive;
does head-butting fawns from windfallen mast.

I don't tell why I've come.
Scanning the winter seascape,
counting strings of bufflehead and goldeneye.
Watchful seals stare back, then dive.

I hike by rainpocked reservoirs,
where tarped dinghies hide behind salal.
I re-find pastures lost in barricades of trees –
sea caves warm with otter spoor and bones.

Over breakfast I mention misjudging
my leap of faith.

Death feeds the forest floor and fungi,
dissolves in ocean depths where worms and dogfish glut.

At the seams between woods and sea
it's hard to miss the customs usual to grief:
condolences, *pro forma* or performative,
the rote rituals of the "funeral home"
(strange phrase) – forced reminiscences.

On the promontory, where sabots lie turtled till summer,
a passing cat halts, listens for mice wintering
in dry grass under the sailboats' shelter.

This is the season:

streams complaining,   carving the swollen beach.
Empty docks moaning   in the damp before dawn.
Spent waves   gulping back over granite.

But much will be renewed.
                              Summer will come,
imaging Eden, the sabots relaunch.
Children will linger by the shoreline till called.

But one will not come, hair stiff from sun-dried swims.
One will not limp home barefoot over barnacles,
lifting palms purpled by blackberries.
One will not loiter collecting crab moults and urchin shells.

What is, is outnumbered by what's not.

The future fills with foreclosed expectations
for one who left no mark or memory to guard,
one ghost we cannot call by name,
one heart we watched once beating in its shell.

Poised on the bare antlers of oaks,
abandoned crows' nests prickle with cinnamon shards
of the summer that once sheltered them.

A wet summer and an idle fall passed by,
scattering the sidewalks with crumbs of rust, sparing
only those dry mementoes snagged on the wicker nests.

And you're also gone, along with everything
except winter. Like an injured dog trying
to crawl away from its own broken flesh, at first

I couldn't face what happened. But I am veined
by your absence, in the same way these oak trees,
outlined by early dusk, vein the winter sky.

PART V

The Salt Worlds

What can anyone say,
speaking of you?
But how sad for those
who say nothing.
Augustine of Hippo, *Confessions*, chapter 3

CINEMATHEQUE

All I really want: to hide between the sheets
of my childhood bed, sleep
until the sun stops coming up.

Could I walk home if I had to,
if things keep getting worse?
Google calculates it's ninety days

by foot, not counting rests. A ferry
pass waits in my wallet in case
I'm broke when I get back

where waves cough and swallow
in stone-hollows along
the nightbound shore,

where water-walking Orion
and his star-map
mirror sparks from plankton

in the sea.
            Rain pops

on the daylit lake. Inflows
oxbow through bulrushes
and bushes of Labrador tea.

Wings shush: three ravens clap
their calls across the lake. Fir boles
catch the ghost sun.

A fawn's skull yellows
in the creek. One by one,
siskins trickle

from fir to fir.
                    Is the internal
world a city or wood? I ask myself
that often, walking

the bag-scraped streets
at night where dead leaves bristle
on municipal trees.

ABIOGENESIS

In the beginning, before home or garden,
our house was unfurnished, the lawn

unsown. At night darkness lay on
naked stones. Cats hunted in the ditch.

> Hazelnut, pine and stonecrop,
> hardhack, hemlock, Sitka willow.

She said *We should have lights* and lights were installed
and she liked the lights so much

we strung Edisons from branch to branch,
planning parties there in summer. We dug

down a lily pond, poured concrete for liner:
the pool spawned mosquitos, reeked

of swamp.

> Bull-kelp, bladderwrack, vulture, eagle,
> eelgrass, guillemot, gull.

Ocean has its own seasons. Winter-clear
saltchuck warming in spring

parturates with green and orange algae

and waves lift, tilting a dugout canoe.

Half high on cedar aerosols
the sprawling fisher thumbs his lines.

Bait hooks jig through mudflats where hulked
in its mansion undersea

Mindless Thing smells fish guts in its
sleep. That creature's nerves once streamed

with sights of a burning landscape
masked in steam – salts and carbon chains

souping ponds in the stone exchanged
their charges and recombined,

micro-mechanisms clicked together,
clicked apart, spinning off

rogue by-products and flawed replicas.
Submarine fissures still nourish

swarming extremophiles, fed on
in their turn by timid worms. Contrived

lights of anglerfish wraith by, luring
abyssal eyes with atavistic fondness

for gleams mimicking moonbeam or meteorite.
That appetite for light has passed to me,

so quickly absorbed in the strobing TV.
Why'd you do that? my manager asks.

I shake my head. He holds me in my tracks
until I'm almost choking on my breath.

Don't know? Because you're scared to death.
So scared I read my iPhone on the train,

gratefully fugue out on ad screens in lifts
instead of looking at the other suits,

afraid of what I'd think of, if I thought.
More than anything I'm afraid of you.

I snail into my whiskies after work,
the joint smoked alone on my backyard stoop.

Afraid of the stain of your silhouette
I bask in the laptop's solace,

drink ego and eros from the twittering net.
The bed smells like musk, mouth bacteria,

piss. *Wash sheets next weekend* I tell myself,
grope at my alarm clock, triple-check it's set.

ZUGZWANG

I sit down for dinner alone at my parents' place.
There's something wrong. I'm cold?

Then I sense what I am: stone sober. But
I know what cupboard holds my parents' booze.

I pour a glass of wine, splash in some kirsch
to help catch up. *That's better,* I think, then:

is this bad? Better not think, eat quick, drink
myself to sleep.
                           Under buzzing auroras

we drowse on the march and bump
each other awake, frozen straps

clacking like spoons.

            That's far enough, Bill Wilson says.
            This is where we sleep.

Outside our tent, a hurricane flocks
north, answering the call of the polycuspid sea.

We inhale, exhale the viscous cold.
Why don't we light the primus I ask, but my friends

say nothing. How long have they been dead?
The polar storm blares, wails

and tilts – another tent pole cracks. Trapped
in our silk mortuary's milky light

I hear below some thumping
in the ice. I slice a vent in our tarpaulin

floor: with knifeblade shave the ice beneath,
excavate a pair of gates that open like

a set of teeth. Sticking my head inside those jaws
I hear sighs, complaints, and soft wails

resounding through the starless atmosphere.
Spirits stir in the windless air, ephemeral

as fog shadows slung by hydro wires.
If you want blood, I call, *my hands are still cut*

from grabbing at beach rocks and barnacles.
But those old nothings barely sway forward

smelling something in my blood they hate.
We've had all we want, they drawl,

*We're sick of living for a moment
and fading away. Feed someone else instead.*

Who? I ask, and see a boy stagger up
wet bluffs towards a lion, happy

to be eaten if the lion had no
other way of loving him. And he

was my secret child, whose body
was broken up and burnt. *Burnt*

with the other garbage, sneer the ghosts.
Is he here, I beg, *is he with you?* but

they keep silent as a heartbeat
in a body you can't touch.

MERCY

In December I'm a maimed buck
in a sea cave, rising and falling on dark
waves, resting torn forelegs in neutral
saltchuck. Then your outline joins the bramble canes
traced black against the cave mouth's arc.

Braced like a *K* inside the arch of rock,
you watch, judging whether I'll heal
or not. Your boots splash into the freezing
water. I lunge for the cloud-scaled ocean
but you catch my antler, and reel

me back. Your voice and fingers shake into
my skin and I surrender – shaking too, drifting
in water past my depth. You push me down
and sea salt singes my eyes and nostrils
shut. I lose the creak of trees sifting

the wind and waves' slap on stone. I lose
the raven's croak and rattle of antlers in the rut's
tangle. But your voice hums along my bones,
mixing your grief with the sea's warble
while water gropes its way into my lungs.

FIRE WORSHIP

What can flesh cherish when winter
unskies the sun? Back late from work

we shave kindling to curls, light them in the pig.
Our cabin's bones are cold. The stovepipe

Rattles, winds stampede from tree
to tree. We lean split fir on cedar

oozing smoke like tea leaves
leaking savour in the pot.

> *Where do you think this carbon's been,*
> *cycling through plant and flesh, and back to air?*

> *Whatever you burn has been burned before.*

Tarred hulls, purple sails. Salt in our hair.

We left Canaan to the slave-host
braying in from the desert

and sailed west, hugging the south coast
till we found a good harbour, rich dirt.

The locals wouldn't sell much ground,
so we asked for just a cowhide's girth

and when they'd gone took a city's worth.
They wouldn't have bargained at all if they'd found

what freighted our ships:
altar bricks to line pit furnaces,

bronze hands held open (fingertips
stained from sacrifices). Child harnesses,

Murex masks and knives for priests.
We consecrated our colony with mixed joy

and grief. Miles inland, a native convoy
smelt burning flesh and thought it was a feast.

> *Whatever you burn has been burned before.*

The widow hesitates by funeral

flames: her uncle tries to reason
with the soldiers: *Our custom is to help*

wives share their husband's pyre.
> *Is it?* An officer

replies, *Our custom is to hang men
like you. Go do your custom, we'll do ours.*

> *Carbon is rarely made or unmade save in stars.*
> *Whatever you burn has been burned before.*

Mauve carpet, taupe seats. She waits with counsel
outside the courtroom. He arrives

just on time. New shades, a pink-striped shirt.
A style he never wore with her.

He goes to salons now, she thinks.
Suddenly a big spender – trying again. He's lucky

we never had kids.

        Whatever you burn has been burned before.

      Remember
that night we fought by the shore? We grabbed

for each other's hips. My foot skidded – you threw
me down the beach. I fell in barnacled

shallows, rolled gasping in the surf.
You splashed down beside me. We both

sat gulping air. Out
on the water's restless blades a staircase

umbilical-like coiled into the sky and spirits
spiralled up and down. You said

        You kicked at me
        in your mother's womb.

I asked what you meant,
alone in the ocean at dawn.

ONCOLOGY OF ICE

Out walking together, I was your old dog
pintoed like shady snow, arthritic,

breath burred by aberrant growths
in my lungs. We found a frozen lake. Fallen snags

lay crisscrossed in its ice, oxblood with sphagnum.
I stared out at the clarified swiftness

of winter sun stroking fronds of snow
across the lake's dark belly. Icebound logs

framed a path to that freedom.
The ice edge creaked beneath my feet.

You called, commanding. But I knew
you'd let it go – figured you'd fake a flash

of anger and forget, hating
to punish. So I went, squinting in doubled

sunlight over deep water.
Then a crack like bones breaking in meat,

and water pulled me down. When I smelt
air again, the water laughed. I fought

to climb out but the white shelf kept shingling
to pieces. As the hole widened, my breath

and flesh cooled. I couldn't get out.
Then you called. Crouched on a log nearby,

smashing ice with a stone, you shouted my name.
I swam to your call – you took hold –

hauled me up trailing broken ropes of cold.
My legs still stiff, I stilted back to shore across the logs.

Safely shuddering through forest
salal, air scratched against the tumours in my chest.

THIRST

In February, creeks are reduced to ice,
dry creek beds and banks burst

with frost-jacks like unclipped claws.
One weekend I go looking for you

on a wooded hillside where underfoot
the slope-scree breaks and sinks. Here

hemlocks grow close,
choking each other for sky. By their trunks

I pull myself uphill, caking hands
with resin and grit. I recognize

your gully from last fall and remember
how, parched from climbing,

I heard you clatter down this thin ravine,
came, filled my dirty palms with you and drank.

Now you're gone. Greenstone in the sike bed
rattles behind me as I climb to the wetland

at the creek's root. In autumn you pooled here
between huge cedars, tinkling like door chimes

as rainwater dripped from the cedar scales above.
Now milky wheels of cat ice lie flat

between the trees, curlicued where eels of air
writhed inside the airtight crust

as inch by inch you sank away.
You vanished into soil,

leaving fossils of your surface
over hollow cups of dirt.

HUNGER

At the end of March the woods wait
for winter to end. Wind breathes

over the fir-tops making
the sound of a dog

blowing wasps off his meat.
And the deer's hunger pains worsen as they hang on

for spring. Winter is outlasting them.
Wandering over rugs of rotten leaves and moss,

they ache for fresh grass, for elder leaves unwinged
from green cocoons. At last the deer find

where you flow darkly through mud beds
under creaking boughs

or trickle silver between fields,
or lie cupped in a swale of stone.

They drink their fill
and sleep and drink again, numbing

their hunger with your weight. Still waiting
for spring, their bodies fall among swordferns

by your banks, or in shelters they find
under fallen logs nearby. Or they slip into your bed,

unravelling slowly in your complicated hands.
I look away from a soggy hide

flapping on a branch in the stream
and snarling, eyeless carcasses

who testify to the cost
of trusting you.

EASTER SUNDAY

On Sunday I stand on the seawall,
looking down at clubs of kelp on your surface,
broken bullwhips hanging behind them.
On the bottom, barnacled riprap

shores up the wall, blotched with rockweed.
Then your surface bulges, tearing yachts
from their wharves, breaking wharves
from their pilings. Charged with silt,

you climb the seawall's face, and roll overtop
in muddy pleats. You slick our streets
with long black tongues. Still swelling, you pour
through buildings, sluicing out downstream windows

like stormflow through a grate. Above the waterline,
bank towers rock back and forth.
As steel shafts in the towers shift,
trapped windowpanes whimper and keen.

Fishing boats washed inland by you
slide rudderless between those complaining mirrors,
and gulls kite overhead, their images
multiplied from building to building. After dark,

tide-rows of burning debris play their flames
on standing water like candles
on volcanic glass. When the eastern sky pales
you seep back towards the coast,

leaving neighbourhoods half buried in black mud.
Spawned by the force of your retreat,
huge whirlpools spin beside
the shoreline like the eyes of baffled gods.

PRINCIPLES OF CONDUCT

"Call no one happy until he's dead"
and even the dead can be unlucky.

Always Mindless Thing in its abyss
hoards catacombs of sailors' limbs,

corridors fogged with crumbs of faulty hearts
one morning halted, dregs

of sour marrow, loam that silted up
sick veins. It plays on loop archival footage

of star entrails spilled on Nagasaki,
human puppets feeding furnaces

with copies of themselves.
                              The lit
world goes on living: whales learn

whalesong from each other.
Rhinoceroses court with gifts

of gazelle racks hooked on their horns. Ants
incurable with cordyceps are carried

from the nest by sisters knowing
never to return. Wolf spiders hunting

through the world's debris
unwind behind them a silken clew

like kids in a labyrinth frightened
of losing the way out.

>   *Where did you come from?*
>   *Where were you when?*

Why won't you leave us alone?
Cobwebs are woven

and swept away, snapweeds spray ripe seeds
as gardeners dislocate their roots.

Its taste is in our mouth. We hide its
egg beneath our tongue. Hating to spit

it out or swallow
we suck it like a candy in our cheek.

I watched a film where frantic
to express the opposite of meaning, a man

holds a woman's gaze and cries:
>   *Kill isn't kill.*

Kill is kiss
Kill isn't kill, it's kiss.

EARTH ON THE OCEAN'S BACK

Rain mists the poppy pins
of passersby outside. In a café,

standing couples rehash the cenotaph
service. Cognoscenti critique beans

and brewing machines while
espresso makers hiss. *I remember*

Mary Battle used to say dreams were false
from spring until saps fell, says an Irish voice

nearby.

                    When did you ever give me what I asked?

Next day my dreams stay with me
through work hours and evening when

I wander through the harbour streets.
Near where the oily tideline sits

a banker searching for a treat
drags on his cigarette and spits.

And how the jealous seagulls' screams
mimic the outbound tanker's horn:

and the urgent sailors' dreams
elaborate their favourite porn.

> *How can I trust you*
> *if you only want what's best*
> *not what I want?*

At an office party, I start with wine,
first red then white: then beer. I'm using

booze like poison. I never drink a cocktail twice,
switch from Rusty Nail to Martini, some

Tiki drink, close out with shots
of rum, tequila. *Kids and kittens,*

don't mix your drinks. I totter home,
open and shut my door without seeing

my cat slide blackly through before it shuts.
In the unlit apartment I shed my shoes,

tumble stunned onto my bed. Next morning
my brain's bruised as badly as I wanted, I'm

verminous. But my cat's missing. I'm terrified
he jumped out the open window, but there's

a notice in the lobby: *Loose cat found*
in stairwell. I bail him out, carry him home

through falling snow. Shops are quickly suffused with carols;
we hear and hum along. Broadcast specials,

baubles, eyesores hype a saint and quasi-child.
Families disband. Vacationers

book flights for Hawaii or Mexico.
Snowbirds unlock their timeshares

in Palm Springs and Sarasota.
Only sleepwalkers populate the north,

addling puddles for drowned artifacts.
For everything that shines is holy, life delights in light –

seedlings in subway tunnels etiolate
white leaves at sunlight dribbling through the grate.

As the naked earth leans into its shadow
skin peels and cracks. We lick sour sips

of blood from lips. How many
infinitesimals does it take to fill

an infinitesimal space? Bleached skies
untether from the earth. I look

down from the dockside and look away.
Some things are too hot to touch, I think.

But not too hot to drink?
No, some things are too hot to drink.

I picture how a bullet would burrow through
my brain or heart, and I'd drop dead,

crumple here in a splash of blood. I imagine walking
calmly from my corpse, like a contract killer.

On weekends I wander till I can't trace back
the way I've come. Feral boys

race down the pavement, windmilling bare arms.
I wait for a car and hitchhike home. There's a point

where trying to understand interferes
with understanding, interpretation

turns to invention. I wake in the middle
of the night in May. The windows are unlit

reflecting the glitter of charge cords
and consoles. When I shift, my skin

jolts on chill cotton that passed the night
untouched.   I squirm my feet

into sneakers still damp
from last night. Shoestrings

whipping nude calves, I jog down
to the dock.

                              Quiet now

the old skidpath's salal, and songless
the sea alders overhanging the pier.

                    Faint lights

flicker under the raft from fluorescent protists
teeming in the mussels' beards.

My footfalls on the float's planking
panic sea perch who corona outwards

in a ring of ephemeral teeth.
Flakes of foxfire ignite and fade

as waves lift the raft and let it drop.
The anchor chains incandesce

as they strain and slack
until the phosphorescence fades. Towards dawn

along the shore, your foam flung up
flashes on black rock and refolds

like the wingbeats of a seabird
        holding its place against the wind.

NOTE TO READER REGARDING
SEXTUS TARQUINIUS

There are obvious limits to what men can add to our conversation about sexual assault and exploitation. So "The Life & Crimes of Sextus Tarquinius" requires some justification.

Media coverage often paints sexual predators as freaks or monsters impelled by perversions alien to the normal male. The implicit assumption (that normal men are incapable of similar sexual misconduct) helps us to distance ourselves (and men we like) from the identified wrongdoers.

However, while that assumption might be reassuring, it strikes me as untrue and unhelpful. I believe that acknowledging and understanding our innate potential for monstrosity is a crucial step towards preventing that potential from being realized. And it seems to me that a man can write about that. So, I have thought it appropriate to write and publish poems portraying the point of view of a normal man who not only commits abnormal crimes but believes his crimes to be entirely excusable.

I have dealt with this subject in the form of myth because in myths, characters have limited control. Myths presume the world will overrule the wishes or aspirations of individuals. Mythopoeia offers a kind of safe space within which we find it easier to admit how little control we have over our lives or even ourselves.

These poems rarely offer the perspectives of the women involved. To the contrary, their perspectives are largely excluded from the protagonist's awareness and consequently from the poems. This is not accidental, and I hope the reader can appreciate why this was necessitated by both my own limitations and the nature of the subject matter itself.

Although "The Life & Crimes of Sextus Tarquinius" is based on reports concerning historical events and figures, it is not factually accurate. My retelling of this popular myth should not be interpreted as a comment upon the character of any real person, or interpreted as a factual account of the historical events on which it is loosely based.

ACKNOWLEDGMENTS

My deepest thanks to all those who commented on earlier versions of these poems, or on the manuscript for this book, especially Jeannine Pitas and Andre Harden. My particular thanks to Anne Franc de Ferrière-Chollat, André Chollat, and Jean-Jacques Franc de Ferrière for correcting the French passages. Everlasting gratitude to my wife, Emily Margaret.

The following poems have been previously published: "Age of Prophecy" and "Earth on the Ocean's Back" in Burning House Press. "Age of Empire" in In/Words anthology *Dis(s) ent.* "Underground," "Walking," and "Cinematheque" in *Barren Magazine.* "Age of Anxiety" and "Age of Experience" in *Train.* "Fire Worship" in *Noise Anthology.* "Age of Innocence" in *Cascadia Rising Review.* "Fugitives Will Bring the News" in *Southword Literary Journal.* "1400 Cromie Rd" in *Arc Poetry.* "Thirst," "Hunger," "Mercy," "It Wouldn't Be Spring," "Counterpoised," and "Departures" in *Prairie Fire.* "Spandrel for Pan Twardowski" in *Freefall.* "Crowsnest Pass," "Vagrants," and "Finisterre" in *CV2.* "Searle's Chinese Room Problem," "Easter Sunday," and "Two Bodies Once" in *Vallum.* "Vancouver Cherries" in *The Dalhousie Review.* "Winter Oaks" in the *Literary Review of Canada.* "The Lotus-Eaters" in *Hart House Review.* More poems appeared in the chapbook *The God of Doors,* published by Frog Hollow Press.

I wish also to acknowledge some of my debts.

"The Lotus-Eaters" takes its name from the poem by Alfred, Lord Tennyson. "Snake in the Mind" takes its title from A.S. Byatt's closing reflections in *Ragnarok.* "Secret Water" takes its title from the book of the same name by Arthur Ransome. "Vagrants" takes its title from a line by Joachim du Bellay. The Antarctic journey described in "Zugzwang" is based on passages from *The Worst Journey in the World,* by A. Cherry-Garrard;

lines about the "starless atmosphere" are paraphrased from *Inferno*, canto III (ll. 22–3); lines about a lion refer to passages in C.S. Lewis's *The Horse and His Boy*, chapter 14. The officer's remarks in "Fire Worship" are paraphrased from remarks attributed to Charles James Napier. The opening two lines of "Principles of Conduct" are paraphrased from Aristotle's discussion of Solon's maxim in *Nicomachean Ethics*, Book I, chapter X (1100a1 l.10 and following).

The film described and very briefly quoted at the end of "Principles of Conduct" is *Pontypool* (2008), written by Tony Burgess, based upon his own novel *Pontypool Changes Everything*, published by ECW Press.

In "Earth on the Ocean's Back," the quote regarding Mary Battle is based on an anecdote told by W.B. Yeats in *Swedenborg, Mediums and the Desolate Places*, and the lines regarding shame being too hot to touch, but drinkable, are drawn from C.S. Lewis's *The Great Divorce*, chapter 8. Also in "Earth on the Ocean's Back," the passage beginning "I wander through the harbour streets …" and the line "For everything that shines is holy, life delights in light" are echoes of William Blake's "London" and *America: A Prophecy* (line 71), respectively.